Family Scrapbook

Going on a Journey
in the 1930s and 40s

Family Scrapbook

Going on a Journey in the 1930s and 40s

Faye Gardner with Anne Callender

Evans

Going on a Journey in the 1930s and 40s

Published by Evans Brothers Ltd in 2006
2A Portman Mansions
Chiltern St
London W1U 6NR

British Cataloguing in Publication Data
Gardner, Faye
Travelling in Grandma's Day (In Grandma's Day)
3. Transportation- Great Britain - History -- Juvenile literature
4. Great Britain - Social conditions - 20th century - Juvenile literature
I Title II Callender, Anne
388'.0941'09044

ISBN 0 237 52904 1
13 digit ISBN (from 1 January 2007) 978 0 237 52904 8

Acknowledgements
Planning and production by Discovery Books Limited
Edited by Faye Gardner
Designed by Ian Winton
Commissioned photography by E.W. Farrelly Photography
Illustrations by Stuart Lafford
This edition published by Evans Brothers in 2006

The publisher would like to thank Anne Callender for her help in the preparation of this book.

For permission to reproduce copyright material, the author and publisher gratefully acknowledge the following:
T. & R. Annan & Sons Ltd, Glasgow: 28; The Automobile Association: 19; Aviation Picture Library: 27; The
Reg Barber Collection: 12; Courtesy of the Board of Trustees of the National Museums and Galleries on
Merseyside: 26 (bottom); the art archive: 21 (left); Glasgow City Archives: 7; 24-25 Glasgow Museums:
Museum of Transport: 11 (top right), 22,24 (left); The Glasgow University Archives & Business Records: cover
(middle right), 26 (top); The Hulton Getty Picture Library Collection Ltd: 9 (top right), 15 (top), 16, 17; The
National Motor Museum, Beaulieu: 14, 15 (bottom), 18; The National Tramway Museum: 7 (top right, bottom
left), 10; The National Tramway Museum (Photographer Glynn Wilton): cover (top left), 11 (bottom left), 12
(top right), 13; The Robert Opie Collection: 8; Science and Society Picture Library: 21 (top right), 23 (top);
W.A.C. Smith: 20.   © Evans Brothers Limited 1997

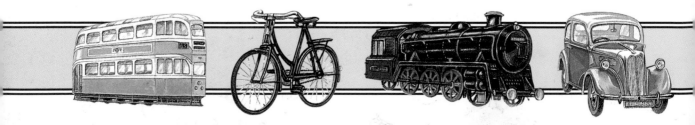

CONTENTS

My name is Anne and I am a grandmother. I have four grandchildren, Karen, Scott, Nicki and Abby.

6

I was born in 1936, before the Second World War. When I was young, I lived on a farm between the towns of Paisley and Glasgow in Scotland.

As you can see from these pictures of Paisley (above) and Glasgow (below), travelling has changed quite a lot since I was a child.

I am going to tell you about the different types of transport we used and some of the journeys we made.

7

'Cycling was safer in those days.'

Bicycles were often the only private transport people could afford. Cycling was safer in those days because there was less traffic about. We saw more bicycles on the roads than cars!

This picture shows you what most bikes looked like then. The handlebars were a different shape to those on modern bikes and most bikes didn't have gears. It was hard work getting up hills!

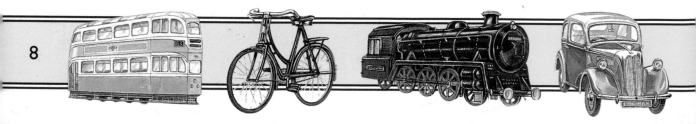

Bicycles were often used by people at work. My dad used his bike to get around the farm. Policemen used bicycles instead of cars to **patrol** the streets.

I got my first bicycle when I was nine years old. It was secondhand. During the war, it had belonged to the **Women's Voluntary Service**. It had big, black handlebars and a very hard saddle. Here I am learning to ride my bike, with the help of my friend Isobel.

I preferred my brother's bike which had shiny, **chrome** handlebars.

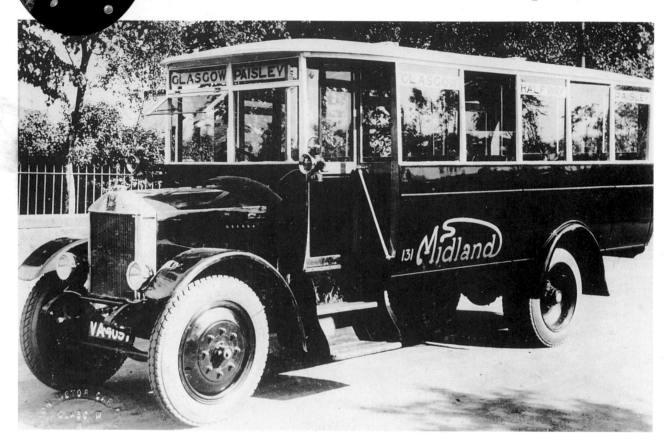

'The bus had wooden seats.'

Every morning I travelled by bus to school in Paisley. I had to walk a mile and a quarter (over two kilometres) to the nearest bus stop.

The bus had wooden seats and there wasn't any heating, so it was cold in winter. It smelt of old cigarettes. In those days smoking was allowed on **public transport**, but smokers had to sit at the back of the bus, or upstairs if it was a double-decker.

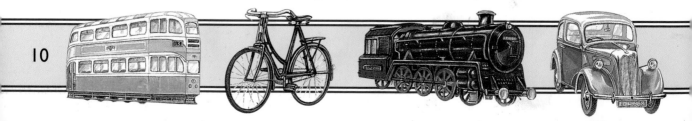

The four-mile (six-kilometre) journey cost one old penny (about 1/2 p). The bus conductor collected passengers' fares into a leather satchel. It was so full of coins that it jingled as he walked up and down the bus.

The bus conductor punched our tickets with a machine like this, which he carried over his shoulder.

The bus was old and often broke down, but I didn't mind. It was a good excuse to be late for school!

People in Glasgow could travel on trolley buses like this one, or by tram, like the one on the next page. Passengers were given tickets that often had adverts printed on the back.

TRY "Ty·phoo" TEA for Indigestion (ask your doctor)

Wh 7920

Trams and trolley buses were powered by electricity from overhead wires. Sometimes the arms that carried electricity to the trolley bus came off the wires. The conductor used a long pole to hook them on again.

Trams drove down the middle of the road on metal tracks. The tracks were kept clean by a 'points cleaner'. He wore a white-topped cap and swept the tracks with a stiff brush. Tram drivers and conductors wore caps with badges like this one.

During the war many jobs on public transport were done by women. They replaced the men who joined the **armed forces**. We called women tram drivers 'motor women'.

13

'You could buy a new car for under £200.'

Most families couldn't afford to own a car. We were lucky because both my parents had a car. My dad had a Rover 12 like this one, and my mum had a Morris 10, like the one on the next page.

You could buy a new car for under £200 in those days. Cars were less comfortable than they are now. They didn't have heaters or radios and the seating was more cramped.

14

This is how many petrol stations looked after the war. There was a shortage of petrol and fewer people could use their cars.

Some cars didn't have **indicators** and drivers had to use hand signals instead. My parents' cars had indicator lights on movable arms that popped out on either side of the car.

'We didn't have any motorways.'

When I was young, roads were smaller and we didn't have any motorways. Road surfaces were rough in many places. It was often a bumpy ride!

People knew less about road safety. There was no **speed limit** on country roads and we didn't have to wear seat belts. In towns, there were no zebra crossings and few traffic lights.

During the war the government ordered road signs to be painted blank or pulled down. This was to stop enemy soldiers finding their way around if they invaded Britain. It made things confusing for ordinary motorists, too!

'Motorbikes were used a lot.'

My dad had a motorbike. Motorbikes were used a lot during the war because they used less petrol than cars.

Motorcyclists wore different clothes in those days. They didn't have to wear a crash helmet: my dad wore a cap and a pair of goggles.

Some motorbikes had sidecars for passengers to ride in. Organisations like the **AA** patrolled the roads using bikes like these. They used sidecars to transport tools and equipment to help motorists who had broken down.

AA men wore smart uniforms and saluted their members if they passed them on the road.

'It was hard to travel long distances.'

Most long journeys were made by steam train. Tickets were cheap and nearly every town and village had a railway station. This is a picture of my local station in Paisley.

The railways are controlled by men in signal boxes along the railway tracks. The signalman in this picture is pulling brass levers that move the **points** on the tracks to make the train change direction.

During the war many trains and railway lines were damaged by bombs. It was hard to travel long distances.

IS YOUR JOURNEY REALLY NECESSARY?

TICKETS

RAILWAY EXECUTIVE COMMITTEE

Trains were often taken over by the armed forces to transport their **troops**. The government asked people to travel less, by putting up posters like this one.

'We sailed to Bute on a paddle steamer.'

Every August we went on holiday to Rothesay Bay on the Isle of Bute. We travelled by steam train to Wemyss Bay, then sailed to Bute on a **paddle steamer** called the *Jeanie Deans*.

On the boat there was a group of musicians who played accordians and fiddles to entertain the passengers. People clapped and sang along to the music.

Sweet Rothesay Bay

LONDON MIDLAND & SCOTTISH RAILWAY.

DONALD A. MATHESON, Deputy General Manager (for Scotland)
ARTHUR WATSON, General Manager

GUIDE BOOK TO ROTHESAY (POSTAGE 2º) FROM A.R.
SECRETARY ADVERTISING COMMITTEE, ROTHESAY

Here I am in Rothesay with my
mum and dad and little sister.
This photo was taken by a
photographer. In those days fewer
people owned cameras: families
on holiday would often pay a
photographer to take their photo.

'We took the ferry across the Clyde.'

On Sunday afternoons my dad drove us to the ice skating rink in Glasgow. We often took the ferry across the River Clyde, because it was quicker than driving all the way around.

This ferry stopped being used in the 1970s, which was when this picture was taken. Underneath the ferry there were huge chains. They stretched across the water to the river bank opposite. These chains stopped the boat from getting swept down the river. They made a terrific clanking noise as the boat moved through the water.

Glasgow was an important port and the River Clyde was a passageway for boats from all over the world. We saw huge cargo ships bringing grain from Australia and tobacco from America.

'Few people travelled abroad.'

When I was young, few people travelled abroad. Making the journey to a foreign country often took many days. Those who could afford to travel abroad mostly went by passenger liner.

Passenger liners were huge steamships that could carry over a thousand people on one journey. A trip to America took at least four days!

Aeroplane travel was rare, too. In those days planes were propeller driven. They were much slower and smaller than modern, jet-powered planes. Flights to countries like Africa and Australia were often made by flying boats like this one.

A flying boat was an aeroplane that could take off from and land on water. They were used because few countries had specially built **landing strips**. A plane like the one in this picture could carry a maximum of sixteen passengers.

'It was unusual to travel far from home.'

When I was small, we travelled far less than we do today. Most of the journeys we made were short ones. It was unusual to travel far from home.

Long journeys were like exciting adventures!

GLOSSARY

AA Automobile Association. An organisation that provides emergency help to motorists who have broken down.

Armed forces The army, navy and airforce.

Chrome A shiny metal.

Indicators The small orange lights on the front and back of a car that flash to warn other traffic when the car turns left or right.

Landing strip An area of ground used by aircraft to take off and land.

Paddle steamer A steamboat with large paddles that push it through the water.

Patrol To travel around a place and inspect it to make sure everything is in order.

Points The rails on a railway track that can be moved to guide a train on to a different line.

Public transport Vehicles like buses and trains that are for everyone to use.

Speed limit The maximum speed that a vehicle is allowed to travel in a certain area.

Troops Organised groups of soldiers who serve in the armed forces.

Women's Voluntary Service A voluntary force of women who helped those suffering from the effects of the war.

OTHER BOOKS TO READ

Other books about 20th-century history for younger readers published by Evans include:

Rainbows *When Grandma Was Young*
Rainbows *When Dad Was Young*
Rainbows *What Was It Like Before Television?*
Tell Me About *Emmeline Pankhurst*
Tell Me About *Enid Blyton*

Britain Through The Ages *Britain Since 1930*
Alpha *1960s*
Take Ten Years *1930s, 1940s, 1950s, 1960s, 1970s, 1980s*

INDEX